YOUR KNOWLEDGE HAS VALUE

- We will publish your bachelor's and
  master's thesis, essays and papers

- Your own eBook and book -
  sold worldwide in all relevant shops

- Earn money with each sale

Upload your text at www.GRIN.com
and publish for free

Michael A. Braun

Did the 'homo economicus' mutate to the concept of behavioural finance and economics?

GRIN Verlag

Bibliografische Information der Deutschen Nationalbibliothek:

Die Deutsche Bibliothek verzeichnet diese Publikation in der Deutschen National-
bibliografie; detaillierte bibliografische Daten sind im Internet über http://dnb.d-
nb.de/ abrufbar.

Imprint:

Copyright © 2006 GRIN Verlag GmbH
Druck und Bindung: Books on Demand GmbH, Norderstedt Germany
ISBN: 978-3-640-18400-2

This book at GRIN:

http://www.grin.com/en/e-book/60829/did-the-homo-economicus-mutate-to-the-
concept-of-behavioural-finance

Freie Universität Berlin

Wirtschaftspsychologie

psychology and economics

Hauptseminararbeit

by

Michael A. Braun

Did the 'homo economicus' mutate to

the concept of behavioural finance and

economics?

Description of relevant findings in psychology and economics

Table of contents

1. Introduction and academic method

Former classic theories mainly strengthened the concept of a 'homo economicus'[1], who behaves economical and exceptionally rational in order to get the maximum advantage for himself. However, as some argue this picture supports not the reality since statistics proof[2] mankind not always behaves rational and economical.[3]

In the past decades, academic research progressed beyond this theory[4], which saw the humans as robots, into the concept of behavioural finance and economics. This acknowledges indeed, people are breathing, sweating, pain-avoiding and pleasure-seeking mammals who have another definition of 'rational' than e.g. computers.[5]

For this, laureate Kahneman worked on the question of how economical decisions could be described if there was no rationality expected at all.[6] In this context, the prospect theory which is assumed to describe people's economical behaviour better than the traditional theories, was developed. Further on, research was undertaken on heuristics, economical framing and anomalies. It was discovered, e.g., persons who feel not sure in their tasks, often disregard the laws of probability and follow their own rules, rather to weigh all potential risks in a rational sense.[7]

So, the essay describes the concept of behavioural finance and economics as well as it is going to check, whether the homo economicus has mutated into it or not. However, although there is criticism[8] on it, the hypothesis is humans <u>are</u> bounded rational and therefore only conditioned able to be described as homo economicus.

To gain more insight, firstly a brief description of the classic theory, observations and of the homo economicus is presented. Later the concept of behavioural finance and economics will be brought in. Secondly main findings in human behaviour will be explained en detail and examples from heuristics, economical framing and anomalies are shown. And finally, a conclusion finalizes the hypothesis up.

---

[1] Klose (1993), pp173 – Individuals act self-oriented and their action is determined by incentives.
[2] Fischer (2005), pp69
[3] Amann (2005), p34
[4] It is also strongly linked with the efficient-markets theory.
[5] The reasons therefore are maybe hormones like dopamine and adrenalin from the limbic system.
[6] As an example, the willingness of consumers to drive long distances for a rebate on relatively cheap products – but not for more expensive ones (!) – was brought up.
[7] Later this will be introduced as 'heuristics'.
[8] The most popular alternative might be, amongst others, the effective market hypothesis.

2. Classical theory in the context of new findings

As part of applied psychology, economic psychology gains access to all relevant aspects of economical life. Therefore, ongoing research is undertaken on the description, application
and prediction of human behaviour in economic contexts.[9]

Now scientists suggest, the homo economicus probably does not have only a 'cold
heart', but discipline / self control are overlapped by feelings and hormones. However, individuals are seen as to be goal-oriented, planning and information-
processing, but with limited capacity. Therefore, when they have alternatives to
choose, they reduce their number and only remaining alternatives are reviewed.[10]

How scientists came to these findings as well as which implications might follow
out of them will be looked at more in depth in the next chapters. On the basis of
historical developments and methods, the rise of a new concept can be observed.

2.1 The evolution of an idea

When economical research became more popular in the end of the 17th century,
economics were closely linked with psychology. Adam Smith, for example, described the principles of individual behaviour on a psychological basis[11]. The drift
off from psychology started when neo-classical economics reshaped the discipline
and gave it an ever more scientific touch. In this time also the concept of the homo economicus was developed and human behaviour was seen as only rational.

Therefore psychology had largely disappeared from economic discussions till the
late 1950s. However, some factors led to the theory of behavioural finance and
economics.[12] Expected personal advantages and discounted-utility models began
to come up. This in turn forced testable hypotheses to be made about the making
of decisions under uncertainty and as well as of inter-temporal consumption.

And during the 1960s and 1970s, in opposition to behaviourist models, cognitive
psychology began to describe the brain as an information processing unit. Leading
psychologists of this field started to test their favoured models against the tradi-

---

[9] Fischer (2005), pp69
[10] Westhoff (1989), p191
[11] This is 'The theory of moral sentiments'. He described a fight between passion and observing.
[12] Hogarth/Reder (1986), pp12

tional economic models of rational behaviour. In 1979 the maybe most important and renowned paper for the development of behavioural finance and economics was written.[13] This extensively used the techniques of cognitive psychology to explain some of the known anomalies in rational economic decision making.[14]

2.2 Basic observations and methods

However, the theory of behavioural finance and economics itself was developed on experimental observations and surveys. In addition, the new 'fMRI'[15] has been successfully used to figure out which brain-areas are active during the process of economic decision making. New was, that especially the areas that are responsible for emotions then became active; overruling the concept of homo economicus.

Experiments[16], which aimed to simulate specific market situations,[17] were seen as being useful to isolate effects of one particular bias. This are systematic changes from the predictions that can be made from a function due to a given response modality (e.g. the assumptions of the phenomena of the homo economicus).

In this regard three mechanisms can be distinguished that bring out biases: (1) social influence, (2) frequency and (3) correspondence.[18] And regardless where a certain time-constraint comes from, humans are facing always a conflict of two contrary aims: (1) to make a good decision and (2) to make it before a deadline.[19]

However, observed behaviour over all could be explained in different ways and to test what's the right one, specific experiments – involving real money! – were designed. Over all, three topics in the concept of behavioural finance and economics are to distinguish[20]: (1) Heuristics, which assume people often decide on the basis of approximate rules of guess, but not on strictly rational analyses.[21] (2) Framing: Here it is argued, the way how a question is presented to the decision

---

[13] Kahneman/Tversky (1979), pp263 to 291
[14] Hogarth/Reder (1986), pp14
[15] Fischer (2005), pp69 – The functional Magnetic Resonance Imaging monitors brain activities.
[16] Fischer (2005), pp69 – e.g. the ultimate or trust game; however, the question of trust and fairness came in when the game was repeated as well as the question of a social environment.
[17] Auctions and the stock market for example.
[18] Roth/Upmeyer (1989), p225
[19] Schürmann (1995), pp36
[20] Shefrin (2002), pp67
[21] Also: cognitive biases and bounded rationality

maker will affect his specific action. And (3) market inefficiencies / anomalies: This tries to explain observed market behaviour, which is neither rational, nor market efficient.

3. The new succeeding concept

Behavioural finance and behavioural economics are two closely related fields. These apply scientific research on social and individual cognitive and emotional biases[22] to the benefit of improved understanding of economic decision making and how it affects markets, prices and the allocation of scare resources.[23] The concept is primarily concerned with the rationality of economic players - or its lack.

Some refer to this twin-area of interest still either as 'behavioural finance' (mainly for behaviour on financial markets) or as 'behavioural economics' (mainly for general economic behaviour). For the sake of ease, and since both combine the disciplines of psychology and economics[24], nowadays many authors do not distinguish any more. Moreover, both explain why / how people make possibly irrational or illogical decisions and value risks when they spend, save, borrow or even invest money.[25] In addition, fear and greed are generally speaking seen as the strongest parameters in the failure of human behaviour at certain markets.[26]

Now the following two sub-chapters are going to (1) describe the concept itself more in depth and moreover (2) are looking at its critics. Both are the basic for the evaluation of the hypothesis in the conclusion chapter later.

3.1 Behavioural finance and economics

Generally speaking, the aim of the new discipline[27] is seen as to get neo-classical economic theory more realistic and according to the actual behaviour of humans.[28]

---

[22] Heuer (2004), p47
[23] Camerer/Loewenstein (2002), pp37
[24] Shefrin (2002), pp21 - Behavioural finance is seen as the study of how psychology affects financial decision making and financial markets and it is a growing area of psychological interest.
[25] Heuer (2004), p47
[26] Amann (2005), pp39
[27] For this research, Daniel Kahneman won himself the Economics Nobel prize in 2002.
[28] Many argue this is evolutionary: In earlier days there was hardly time for rational calculations.

However, the assumption of many economists is still that markets reach on the long run rational outcomes despite the irrational behaviour of some participants. Also standard economics assumes each person has certain stably and well-defined preferences, and that these are tried to be maximized rationally. Therefore these economists assume people behave extremely rational, which they do not. Furthermore, human deviations from rationality often are systematic. For this the new discipline relaxes traditional assumptions by incorporating such observable and systematic differences from rationality into the economic standard models.[29]

How else could massive speculative bubbles such as the Dutch tulip mania in the 17th century, the temporary over-evaluation of stocks in 1929 and 1987, as well as the boost of junk bonds (especially in the Americas; but for different reasons) in the 1980s and, not to mention, the Tech-Bubble at the turn of the millennium be explained?[30] These occasional scenarios of dramatic wins in value followed by incredible losses are hard to interpret on a rational basis. Therefore psychology and the concept of behavioural finance and economics are seen to help out well.

But how does it come, that humans who are seen as being rational still display limitations and complications? Maybe market-forces, individual learning and evolution leave these qualities irrelevant?[31] Probably not, since people show such behaviour also in other economical contexts.[32] Moreover, one can think of bounded rationality, which will be looked at more in depth later, instead. This reflects limited cognitive abilities that constrain the problem solving process of humans. Also bounded will-power might explain why people sometimes decide in a way that cannot be in their long-run interest at all. Further on, some argue these mistakes often are repeated because individuals are not always fully informed.[33]

To gain broader insight in this, researchers have worked on certain behavioural principles[34] such as the prospect theory (see later detailed along with some others),

---

[29] Rabin (1998), pp11 to 46
[30] In these entire scenarios one could find certain assets that gained up to 1,000 percent or even more, but later lost also more than 90 percent – both without any fundamental and rational reason.
[31] Goldberg/Nitzsch (2000), pp259 and also pp273
[32] Barber/Odean (1999) - E.g. two mistakes investors often make: excessive trading and the tendency to disproportionally hold losing investments while selling winners. These systematic biases seem to have their origins in human psychology. The tendency for human beings to be overconfident causes the first bias in investors, and the human desire to avoid regret prompts the second.
[33] Goldberg/Nitzsch (2000), pp25
[34] Shleifer (2000), pp19

cognitive dissonances, anchoring, overconfidence, heuristics and gambling behaviour / speculation, magical thinking (in terms of stock market prognosis e.g. oracle of Delphi and astrology), attention anomalies and global culture.

Most of these boundaries seem be watched nowhere better than on financial markets.[35] The flood of information leads everyone to try to get at least little understanding of what is going on.[36] However, like Quixote's fight against windmills there is hardly any chance to manage all information that's available. And therefore individuals have to select which causes selective attention – and often leads to self-fulfilling prophecies. A phenomenon that is vital all the time, since it is mostly possible to frame certain decision problems in more than one way. Alternative frames may be compared to alternative perspectives on a visual scene.[37]

On the basis of behavioural finance and economics the newly developed models are addressed now to particular observed anomalies and to modify standard neoclassical models. They describe humans as using heuristics and being affected by framing effects. Although it seems to be the nature of humans to view these conclusions as just another indication of how dumb everyone, rather one self is, behavioural finance and economics is now a significant part of the economical framework; though it doubts – or at least questions – rational human behaviour.

Nevertheless it was empirically proven people behave consistently irrational,[38] there is still criticism. Therefore especially the concept of the effective market hypothesis is assumed to give an alternative answer. This however has not shown that the homo economicus has survived, but the new concept even strengthened.

3.2 Criticism on behavioural finance and economics

The critics usually support the efficient market theory and argue, behavioural finance and economics is rather a mix of anomalies than real science - and these eventually will be priced out anyway.[39] Moreover, rather than being science, the

---

[35] This is the reason why most examples in the essay rely on / link with this financial topic.
[36] Goldberg/Nitzsch (2000), pp10
[37] Kahneman/Tversky (1985), pp25
[38] Kahneman/Tversky (2000); pp2
[39] Mandelbrot/Hudson (2004), pp57 – But: it's almost not possible to be better than the market.

new concept often stands accused of consisting of only little more than anomalies-data mining followed by the search for a fitting behavioural explanation.

The theoretical foundations of the efficient market theory were laid in the 1960s[40] when it was assumed, the buyer of a certain good acts rational in making this purchase, which in turn will eventually result in a change of prices. From then, it has become the central theory in finance for nearly 40 years.

In the classical assumption the hypothesis defined efficient financial markets as some in which prices always fully reflect all available information.[41] Although statistical evidence was found in the beginning, new studies have reversed parts of the evidence and they now emerged as an alternative view on financial markets.[42]

The hypothesis rests on three arguments[43] which rely on each other as well as on some rather weak assumptions: (1) investors are seen to be rational and therefore to value securities (e.g. stocks, bonds) rationally, (2) to the extent that some are not rational, their trades are random and hence cancel each other out without effecting prices and (3) to the extent that many are irrational in similar ways, they are met in the market by rational players who eventually eliminate their influence.

However, if behavioural finance and economics really are to replace the hypothesis as the most accepted one, it is not sufficient to simply find interruptions with the latter. Evidence and theory tell the same: financial markets are inefficient, just as an economist would expect. Moreover, once one sees markets as places where different types of humans – some rational, some not – interact, and understands the forces that shape their demands, one can think about many new problems.[44] So, another criticism on the new concept is that by choosing which bias to emphasise, one can predict either under-reaction or over-reaction. Thus, one finds a story to fit all the facts and explain a phenomenon – or to find right the opposite fact.

---

[40] Samuelson (1965), pp512
[41] Shleifer (2000), pp1
[42] Shleifer (2000), p2
[43] ibid
[44] Shleifer (2000), p197

Moreover some critics support, cognitive theories are models of decision making, not of economic behaviour in general. Therefore it is only applicable to once-off decision problems that are typically presented to participants of experiments or in surveys. And the observed behaviour in an experiment therefore is not necessary applicable to any given situation on a market. For this, the traditional gild of scientists is sceptical in general of experiments and surveys.[45] They demand research has to be designed to avoid biases, lack of motivation or even strategic behaviour.

Overall, one finds a lot criticism on the new concept. But what if it is still right?

4. Prospect theory: main findings in human behaviour

Baring the hypothesis from the beginning in mind, one might assume latter criticism to be wrong. The concept of humans acting rational and reasonable (homo economicus) seems to be overcome. Though few psychological concepts found their way in the field of economics; still some psychologists were able to make a contribution that has had a major influence on the contemporary economic theory. For this, the 'prospect theory' is an excellent example of academic creativity[46]; although theoretical findings were not new, but they are a mix of known elements.

Developed in 1979 and backed by strong empirical evidence, the theory first described how individuals evaluate losses / gains.[47] From that point on, certain behaviour observed in economics could be explained referring to the prospect theory, which basically is divided into two stages: editing and evaluation. As an example, one might think of the lottery: a win of 100 is good, but a million would be better. And a win of a million and 100? What is the additional use of the 100? Does it then really matter having 100 more / less? No, but in the first case it does.

---

[45] However, others claim that results usually are reproducible in various situations and countries and often do lead to good insight human behaviour.
[46] Kahneman/Tversky (1979), pp263 to 291
[47] Originally the term 'prospect' referred to 'lottery'.

A topic of the prospect theory is the way in which humans frame economic out-come or transactions in their mind and how this affects the utility they expect to receive. Especially this has widely been used in behavioural finance and econom-ics – and the results are not at all in favour of the homo economicus. Framing and prospect theory were applied to a range of situations which appear to be inconsis-tent with standard economic rationality such as the status quo bias, various gam-bling and betting games, inter-temporal consumption and the endowment effect.[48]

Put it simple, what the theory says is that humans often / usually go for a relative rather than an absolute judgement.[49] Regardless, this has rich implications on the economic behaviour of humans. And importantly the theory is based on substan-tial empirical backing from a large number of experiments and other research.

Although many humans constantly follow judgemental errors[50], they still can be educated and therefore overcome these errors by time. At least there is evidence that once a person is informed / trained, she tends to decide more in line with ra-tional behaviour and then makes more often a rational choice.[51] Also, humans tend to learn, and competition has an influence on the emergence of rational behaviour.

Overall, three major areas divide and dominate behavioural finance and econom-ics. These are: heuristics, framing and anomalies[52]. At the main findings within theses areas will be looked at in the following. Further on, certain specific psycho-logical behaviour is described more clearly. Still, due to focus and to get the point over, not every single type of behaviour can be explained. Phenomena like: parts of over-confidence (about own knowledge / abilities), conservativism[53], selective attention, illusion of control and regret avoidance arise, too, are missing here.

---

[48] Kahneman/Tversky (1979), pp263 to 291 – The all will be looked at more in depth later.
[49] Kahneman/Tversky (1984), pp341 to 350
[50] Investors often have the irrational tendency to sell their winners to secure profits, but keep losers to avoid real losses. This causes them to sell too early when markets go up, but too late when they go down. Maybe this comes from the feeling that pain of loss is stronger than pleasure of gain.
[51] Shiller (2004), p12
[52] Although other sources sometimes distinguish differently between theses mentioned areas (such as: heuristics are also mental accounting and anchoring); this essay is assuming this distribution.
[53] In this case it means humans tend to stick with older opinions rather than adapt new findings. Therefore it might be linked with the endowment effect / status quo bias, but is slightly different.

4.1 Heuristics

Theoretically speaking, this is a methodological procedure for discovering suit-
able solutions to any given problem.[54] The principle feature of heuristics therefore
is the formulation of an investigation on a specific question. Then the working
hypothesis serves to direct the course of the investigation, and is modified and
redefined as relevant facts are discovered and analyzed. During the investigation,
the heuristic reduces the range and increases the plausibility of possible solutions.
Over all, the concept of heuristics has played a fundamental role in the acquisition
of scientific knowledge, since it provides a good result with less effort. And in
fact, it is an essential component of many forms of complex human behaviour. [55]

Applied to the concept of behavioural finance and economics, heuristics can be
thought of as rules of thumb that one uses to make decisions.[56] So, when it comes
to deciding, humans rely on their personal view, no matter how imperfect it actually is. Consequently, in contrast to the concept of the reasonable and ideal homo
economicus who is always up to maximise his prospective value, heuristics could
lead to suboptimal decisions. To understand the issue more clearly, e.g. one could
ask a number of people whether a stroke or murder does kill more people. Then
many will think of the tales of crimes they read or saw on the news and answer,
more die of homicide. This is known as 'availability heuristics' because it bases
decisions on the available information.

Generally speaking are heuristics certain individually developed methods to reduce the felt complexity of a situation / question and to get a fast solution on that.

4.1.1 Loss aversion

Loss aversion describes the tendency of people to prefer to avoid losses than to
acquire additional wealth.[57] Some studies suggest this part of prospect theory is
psychologically twice as powerful as looking for higher gains. And this leads to

---

[54] Strickland (2001), p303
[55] ibid
[56] Shefrin (2002), pp32
[57] Kahneman/Tversky (1979), pp263 to 291

risk aversion when people evaluate possible gains. Loss aversion could be observed very well in investor behaviour such as the unwillingness to sell badly performing shares. If doing so one would have to change a nominal into a real loss.

Further on, whether a potential buy includes a loss or a gain is important to humans and the business world, too. The question is if one would rather get a discount or avoid a surcharge of the same amount. The same price change is seen differently and therefore has a significantly different effect on individual consumer behaviour. Although traditionalists in the field of economics would consider this and all other effects of loss aversion to be completely irrational, it is even more important to marketing and the concept of behavioural finance and economics.

However, can the avoidance of losses really be irrational? The implicit assumption of traditional economics is that the only relevant measurement is the absolute vs. the relative change in expenditure. As an example,[58] saving ten percent on a certain good is considered to be equivalent to avoid paying ten percent extra (e.g. a surcharge or fee) – although a discount is not equivalent to avoiding a surcharge.

For better understanding, one could imagine any item with an original cost of 100 units. A certain buyer is expecting to pay this, but then is offered a discount of ten percent by the shop. Therefore the price now would be 90 units, which means an absolute and a relative saving of ten units and percent. On the other side one might think of a, usually mandatory, shop surcharge or fee of the same amount and the buyer therefore would have to pay 110 units. Avoiding or getting this as a gift, however, would only mean coming back to the original price. Despite this, the buyer sees such action as a saving for him. Thus the price is on what he was expecting to pay anyway, but the perceived saving of ten units is only some 9.09 instead of ten percent.

---

[58] Kahneman/Tversky (1991), pp1039 to 1061

Regardless the obvious worse outcome, but according to many studies, buyer prefer the latter action to the first one[59] (if they do not see the exact but percentage figures). When the amount of savings relative to the remaining money is different, the value of the buy changes soon. When using this example, decisions made by consumers are irrational by any means. In addition, it often has been tested that the effect of relative evaluation as shown is more obvious the greater the potential amount saved is relative to the total amount the decision-maker has to spend.[60]

4.1.2 Gambler's fallacy

Humans tend to evaluate and reason probabilities and chances constantly wrong, which is considered to be a logical fallacy. And therefore, e.g. the gambler's fallacy is one of many misunderstandings which arise in everyday life. For scientists, this fallacy is a cognitive bias that is produced by a psychological heuristic which is called the 'representativeness heuristic'.

And although it could be applied to any form of gambling, it is easiest to illustrate the gambler's fallacy by considering coin-tossing. Usually humans believe that if a flipped coin came, say, three times in a row with the number up, it is now more likely not to do so again. Similarly, just because a stocks / goods market has gone up or down for a while does not mean, it now is going the other way soon.[61]

Anyway, back to the example: The gambler's fallacy could be illustrated by a little example in which a coin is tossed again and again. As a precondition one has to suppose that the coin is fair and the chance to come up with a head is exactly fifty-fifty. Then the chance to come up heads twice after another is 0.5 times 0.5, which one fourth and three times would be one eighth.

Hence if a coin is flipped 20 times and comes up with the head every time. What is the probability it will come up with the number the next time? Of course 0.5, as seen above. In real life, however, if a coin is tossed 20 times and the result always is heads, it is far more likely that there is something wrong with the coin than the game is honest. And not only people who belief in the concept of the homo eco-

---

[59] Kahneman (1991), pp193 to 206
[60] Kahneman/Tversky (1991), pp1039 to 1061
[61] Goldberg/Nitzsch (2000), pp74

nomicus would argue that it is far more likely that coin is manipulated, than that the initial premise is correct and the next toss will be fifty-fifty for heads.

However, mathematically speaking, the probability is equal one that heads eventually will be equal to numbers. Therefore a gambler who spends money will be able to return to his starting point over time. However, the expected number of times to play is infinite, and so is the expected amount of capital that is needed. Therefore, gambler fallacy clearly seems to be a malfunction in human behaviour.

4.1.3 Self-serving bias / Self-attribution Bias

As seen above, humans are not always acting rational[62], but often very human. For example, they are also more likely to claim responsibility for their successes than their failures.[63] This is when a self-serving bias or self-attribution bias occurs.

An example might be marking in schools or universities: If one got a good or very good mark, he would argue this is his own success. If one does poorly instead, he is more likely to say it was the teachers fault – or just bad luck. However, applied to a general situation, this behaviour hinders a person in two ways: (1) one does not learn from a particular mistake, since it is not even seen as a mistake. And (2) a person feels himself like being a smart or qualified person when he is just lucky.

The ultimate result of this bias might be any given negotiation in which every side might interpret the situation to their own. The parties even may completely refuse to continue the communication, since they might believe the other side does not play the game fair and therefore needs to be punished.[64]

In addition there is a group-serving bias which is a similar bias, but on the group level. People tend to interpret any certain information they receive in a way that is beneficial to their interests. So one could argue, people are likely to claim external

---

[62] Like in the way the concept of the homo economicus would suggest to act.
[63] Miller/Ross (1975), pp213 to 225
[64] Babcock/Loewenstein (1997), pp109 to 126 - There is a lot experimental evidence to this: When parties have to negotiate a fair agreement, the evaluations depend on to which side one belongs to. This however, the homo economicus would not do. He instead would look for a real fair outcome.

causes for their performance and a self-serving bias simply is a form of wishful thinking (as seen later) of how things could or should, have been – but not are.

4.2 Framing

Another important concept in behavioural finance and economics is the one of 'framing'. It describes the fact that the way an individual 'frames' any transaction in his mind will determine the utility she receives or expects.[65] This concept is part of the prospect theory and mental accounting uses it for the analyses, too.

In economical contexts, framing means the way in which any given rational choice question is presented or framed. Inventors e.g. base their decisions on the way they frame a specific problem or percept risk, which is one of the most intriguing areas in behavioural finance.[66] This framing, however, takes place through a variety of mental and emotional factors that vary from person to person.[67] Framing biases, however, affect all kinds of areas in the field of behavioural finance and economics such as investing, lending and also borrowing decisions.[68]

It was shown that the way how framing is done, indeed does affect the solution or outcome (i.e. the final choice one goes for) on the question. In systematic reversals of preference, scientists described the very same problem in two ways, but got significantly different answers.[69] Although the two solutions were – in the end – absolutely identical, the change in the wording between the two, lead the participants to decide different. Maybe because they also use mental accounting …

---

[65] Goldberg/Nitzsch (2000), pp90
[66] Shleifer (2000), p181
[67] Shefrin (2002), pp36
[68] Kahneman/Tversky (1986), pp2 – … and they strongly contradict the traditional rational choice.
[69] Kahneman/Tversky (1981), pp453 to 458 – A good example would be the question: 'Would you prefer to buy two bottles of milk, but getting one bad in the fridge? Or do you instead prefer forgetting one of the two in the shop at the counter? Same result, but different ways to get there …

4.2.1 Mental accounting

As seen above, this is another strong contradiction to the homo economicus.[70] It focuses on the question why humans sometimes separate decisions that should, in principle, be combined. For example, many people have a designated household budget for food of all kinds at home and one for going out. However, they will not eat a nice lobster at home, because this would be more expensive than a simple fish. Instead they are likely to order the lobster in a restaurant even though the cost there is even higher. If people instead would turn it the other way round and eat fish in restaurants and lobster at home, they would save money.

More theoretically speaking mental accounting, therefore, describes the process when people categorise and evaluate economic outcomes (as a percentage of a basic value).[71] Theorists argue that people put their assets into a number of mental accounts and mentally frame these as belonging to their current income, their current wealth or their future income. Nevertheless the accounts are still separated.[72]

4.2.2 Anchoring

The term 'anchoring' is used in the field of psychology to describe the human tendency to rely on just one piece of information (or a basis-figure) when it comes to making a certain decision. People than tend to anchor only on this information. Usually once the anchor is set, yet, there is now a strong bias towards it.

An example would be, if one is asked to think (1) of a certain, personal number and then (2) to estimate the number of, say, citizens of India. Although there hardly might be any relation between these numbers, humans are most likely to link the two and then guess for the second number something next to the first. Just the simple fact, having thought of this number influenced them for the second.

Therefore the concept of anchoring is strongly influencing economical live, too. Say, if an individual has set a frame in mind, or anchored on something, the indi-

---

[70] This applies at least in a way since reducing complexity does not necessarily mean being not rational. However, only the way and how it is processed seems to be not always rational.
[71] Thaler (1980), pp39 – Separation is done in certain mental accounts from which the name is.
[72] Goldberg/Nitzsch (2000), pp90 – 'Liver-worst' example: Imagine one is about to buy a household machine at shop A for 2.000 or at the more away B for 1.990. Most would decide for A. If one instead has to buy a piece of liver-worst away for 2 or nearer for 7, most would walk to the 2!

vidual then is no longer open to another rational solution.[73] Therefore, if this concept is seen as being correct, the traditional economic model of rational choice and the homo economicus with his all-time rationality has to be wrong.

4.3 Anomalies

Market-wide anomalies generally cannot be explained by individuals that are suffering from cognitive biases since individual biases not often have a big enough effect to change prices. In addition, individual biases even could potentially cancel each other out. Cognitive biases have real anomalous effects only if there is a social influence with an emotional content (e.g. greed, fear), leading to phenomena such as herding and group-actions[74]. Behavioural finance and economics therefore rest not only on social psychology but also on individual psychology.

There are two exceptions to this generalization. First, it might be the case that enough individuals (critical mass) become biased and act different from rational expectations. Then such behaviour became the norm and it gets market-wide effects. Second, small but significant groups could have a strong influence, too.[75]

4.3.1 Endowment effect & status quo bias

Another contradiction to the homo economicus is the endowment effect[76] which is that people value a certain property / good even more once their rights to it have been established. In other words, people value it more as soon as they own it.[77] In an experiment, people demanded a higher price for something they acquired recently; but put a lower price on a substitute to it which they did not own.[78]

The endowment effect therefore, again, is different to the standard economic theory which would assume that a person is willing to pay the same price as she would accept as compensation once the good is to sell. And especially if people

---

[73] Same applies at a court. Although certain information might be officially cancelled by the judge; it still will stay in peoples, journalists and others minds to be remembered by time.
[74] Although one could think of a big hype such as the Dutch tulip-mania which was an anomaly.
[75] Here one could think of young, innovative and tech-oriented individuals with money to spend.
[76] Kahneman/Tversky (1974), pp1124
[77] Goldberg/Nitzsch (2000), pp131
[78] Thaler (1980), pp39

are the heir of something or possessed it for a long time, they tend to have a very strong commitment to this good – and a low will to sell it at all. In this regard the status quo basically means to have everything (property) remaining as it is.[79]

This however applies not only to goods, but also to the whole individual person.[80] One wants to stick with a certain product (brand) or the way of doing things as he has done it for ages.[81] This idea is called status quo bias and is part of the endowment effect; in general people like things to stay relatively the same and value things they posses more.[82] The reason for this is because one values disadvantages of changing things more negatively than advantages of changing things positively. In addition, one might start thinking that things might be not that bad anyway.[83]

Although the existence of both – endowment effect and status quo bias – is often questioned by economists, the effects are, if they are true as assumed here, a vital economic phenomenon since behaviour, prices and decisions are influenced.

4.3.2 Life cycle & inter-temporal consumption

Another concept that focuses on the ideal world (but also on human limitations) is the economic theory of inter-temporal consumption. This idea is trying to explain people's preferences on how to consume and to save ideally over their lifetime.

In the 1950s the homo economicus-style life-cycle model[84] was built on how income distribution problems arise over the circle of life. This assumes that everyone spends / consumes a defined amount of his expected lifetime income at every point in life. Thus, the annuities are expected to be more or less the same. This also would mean people have to borrow against their future at study- and early working-life when their income is low. Also their savings will be bigger during their most productive working years. And finally during retirement they consume the savings. Unexpected gains (like heirs, lottery) would be treated like an income increase, the normal annuity would be consumed and the rest would be saved.

---

[79] Goldberg/Nitzsch (2000), pp131 to 134
[80] Kahneman/Tversky (1979), pp263
[81] This effect can be seen mostly when it comes to technical products. (e.g. cars, computers) The brand of the first car for example has a strong influence on later car purchases.
[82] Samuelson/Zeckhauser (1988), pp7 to 59
[83] Goldberg/Nitzsch (2000), pp131 to 134
[84] Which was is mainly the work of laureate Milton Freeman et al.

Although the theory sounds convincing; most individuals seem not to care about that – but the concept of behavioural finance and economics might explain why: The difference between the predicted and the real behaviour is that the annuities and they way how they are treated are not distributed flat but are spent in waves. Therefore an average-person consumes not enough in his early and late life[85] but strongly too much (compared to the annuity) during the earning years and not enough once he is old for the purpose to give something to the kids.

Statistics and research shows that people mentally divide their assets into mental accounts (see 4.2.1) such as the current income and assets (savings) as well as the future income. This explains why individuals usually consume more when they have more: in the years with the highest earnings. Therefore they contradict the proportional annuity-assumption of the life-cycle model and a homo economicus.

4.3.3 Overoptimism & wishful thinking

In combination with the self-serving and self-attribution bias, overoptimism suggests humans tend to be too optimistic / confident about themselves.[86] Therefore most individuals have unrealistic views of their abilities and their knowledge. And many think for example, they know above average how to drive, have a better sense of humour or how to get along with others. Also a systematic planning fallacy can be viewed since many humans assume their tasks will be finished sooner than they actually are.[87] Also when students were asked whether they will perform better than he average, most will say yes – but the result often is different.

To be clear, this is also linked with wishful thinking, although not in the way of a self-fulfilling prophecy. And since investing is a social activity,[88] investors for example spend a substantial part of their leisure time discussing investments, reading of it or gossiping about others successes / failures in investing, they are

---

[85] This is because he might not want to borrow against potential future earnings, but also fails to save enough to finance an adequate retirement. Also windfall gains are not handled adequately.
[86] Kahneman/Tversky (2000), pp2
[87] Goldberg/Nitzsch (2000), pp131 to 134
[88] French/Roll (1993), pp219

also the ones to become victims of wishful thinking easily.[89] And bearing this in mind, can anyone say this is what the homo economicus-concept originally said?

---

[89] Shiller (1993), pp167

5. Conclusion and assessment of the hypothesis

As argued previously, neo-classical theories – the 'cold' ones that came after Adam Smith et al – strongly favoured the concept of a rational and calculating 'homo economicus'. Although there is evidence that this concept has a good theoretical foundation and is valid once humans use their brains with intention, nowadays many cognitive psychologists argue this idea is not a hundred percent correct anymore. They instead see the humans as being more natural, human and controlled by feelings than a person with a homo economicus-view would think.

So, from the 1970s to today the prospect theory together with the joint neuropsychological-economical concept of behavioural finance and economics has arisen. And this happened not only on personal experiences, but also through surveys, tests and observations as well as with the support of the brain-watching fMRI-technique. In turn, it has lead researchers to findings how humans as an individual really act and proceed when it comes to (economical) cognition and actions. So, one finding of the behavioural concept also is why people constantly miscalculate risks and returns as well as they are not always able to understand time-effects.

However, although there is criticism and contrary ideas on that (such as the efficient market hypothesis), the hypothesis of the essay was humans <u>are</u> bounded rational and therefore only conditioned able to be described always as a homo economicus. Therefore to gain insight, a theoretical introduction on the homo economicus and recent observations of efficiency in human action and rationality were given. Also the concept of behavioural finance and economics was explained and findings in human behaviour were discussed together with some examples.

One might be the one of how irrational individuals are in the willingness of an average consumer to drive long distances for a small percentage rebate on relatively cheap products – but not for more expensive ones (!). Also the speculative market bubble at the time of the Dutch tulip mania in the 17th century was discussed. For such misbehaviour the reasons as well as the explanations are countless. The ones that have been given most however are evolutionary. Researchers favour the idea humans are bounded rational since this works faster than calculating everything.

Over all it can be stated behavioural finance (which is the more specialized part of the concept) and economics (the more general economical part) have become widely accepted. This now is neither a subdiscipline of something, nor just a new paradigm. Instead it tries to improve existing models to a more realistic approach.

On the basis of behavioural finance and economics the developed models are now addressed to particular observed anomalies and for the modification of standard neo-classical models. They describe humans as using heuristics and being affected by framing effects. Although it seems to be the nature of humans to view these conclusions as just another indication of how dumb everyone, rather one self (!) is, behavioural finance and economics is now a significant part of the economical framework; though it doubts – or at least questions – rational human behaviour.

Put it simple, what the theory says is that humans for time reasons and to reduce complexity often / usually have to go for a relative rather than an absolute judgement. Therefore the concept of homo economicus has to be wrong in these special cases like the hypothesis suggested – or has mutated into the concept of behavioural finance and economics. And since this theory has substantial empirical backing, this now has great implications on the economic behaviour of humans.

But there is hope: although many humans constantly follow judgemental errors like selling winner stocks e.g. but sticking to their loosers, they still could be educated and overcome these returning errors and misbehaviours. At least there is evidence that once a person is informed and trained, she then tends to decide more in line with rational behaviour and goes then more often for the rational choice.

Although the essay could give only a brief insight on both, the concept of the homo economicus and the concept of behavioural finance and economics, there still are loads of questions left open since it is a rather new field of interest. Mainly the question whether the latter has really outplaced the other seems still to be unanswered. Nevertheless, the hypothesis that the concept of behavioural finance and economics definitely and only has outplaced the homo economicus seems to be, with the support of many examples in the categories of heuristics, framing and anomalies, not true. Instead both are linked and seem to interact since humans <u>are</u> bounded rational but also <u>are</u> able to calculate and act rational.[90]

---

[90] This assumption is what laureate Gary S. Becker found out and got honoured for. He extended the concept of the homo economicus on the general life – and argued both concepts are linked.

Abstract

Former classic economic theories mainly strengthened the concept of the 'homo economicus', who strongly behaves economical and rational. Nowadays however, some argue this supports not the reality, and so academic research progressed. For this, laureate Kahneman et al developed the prospect theory which is assumed to describe people's economical behaviour better than traditional theories.

Therefore the essay elaborates on the concept of behavioural finance and economics as well as it checks, whether the homo economicus has mutated to this. However, although there is criticism, the hypothesis is humans <u>are</u> bounded rational and therefore only conditioned able to be described as homo economicus.

To gain insight, a brief introduction on theory, homo economicus and recent observations of efficiency in human action and rationality is given. Later the concept of behavioural finance and economics is brought in and findings in human behaviour are discussed together with examples from heuristics, economical framing and anomalies. Finally, an assessment of essay and hypothesis sums all up.

List of references

1.   Amann (2005): Amann, C., *Angst und Gier gebannt in Kurven – Psychologie spielt eine entscheidende Rolle*, Süddeutsche Zeitung Nr. 241, München 19.10.2005

2.   Babcock/Loewenstein (1997): Babcock, L., Loewenstein, G., *Explaining Bargaining Impasse: Role of Self-Serving Biases*, Journal of Economic Perspectives, 11/1, Cambridge 1997

3.   Barber/Odean (1999): Barber, B., Odean, T., *The Courage of Misguided Convictions*, Financial Analysts Journal, issue 6/99, Charlottesville 1999

4.   Camerer/Loewenstein (2002): Camerer, C., Loewenstein, G., *Behavioural Economics: Past, Present, Future*, Princeton 2002

5.   Fischer (2005): Fischer, M., *Ins Schwarze treffen - Mit neuen Methoden erkunden Ökonomen die Grundlagen menschlichen Verhaltens*, Wirtschaftswoche Nr. 28, Düsseldorf 07.07.2005

6.   French/Roll (1993): French, K., Roll, R., *The arrival of information and the reaction of traders*, in: Thaler, R. (editor), Advances in behavioural finance, Russell Sage, New York 1993

7.   Goldberg/Nitzsch (2000): Goldberg, J., von Nitzsch, R., *Behavioural Finance – Gewinnen mit Kompetenz*, 3. Edition, FinanzBuch Verlag, München 2000

8.   Heuer (2004): Heuer, S., *Affe mit gutem Pressesprecher – Interview mit Colin Camerer*, McK – McKinsey Wissen Nr. 07, Verlag brandeins, Hamburg 2004

9.   Hogarth/Reder (1986): Hogarth, R., Reder, M., *Editors' Comments: Perspectives from Economics and Psychology*, Journal of Business, Chicago 1986

10. Kahneman/Tversky (1974): Kahneman, D., Tversky, A., *Judgement under uncertainty – Heuristics and biases*, Science Nr. 185, Washington 1974

11. Kahneman/Tversky (1979): Kahneman, D., Tversky, A., *Prospect Theory - An analysis of decisions under risk*, Econometrica Nr. 37, Blackwell, New York 1979

12. Kahneman/Tversky (1981): Kahneman, D., Tversky, A., *The framing of decisions and the psychology of choice*, Science 211, Washington 1981

13. Kahneman/Tversky (1984): Kahneman, D., Tversky, A., *Choices, Values and Frames*, American Psychologist, 04/84, Washington 1984

14. Kahneman/Tversky (1985): Kahneman, D., Tversky, A., *Frame of decisions and the psychology of choice*, in: Wright, G., (editor) Behavioural Decision Making, Plenum, New York 1985

15. Kahneman/Tversky (1986): Kahneman, D., Tversky, A., *Rational choice and the framing of decisions*, Journal of Business, volume 59, issue 4, Chicago 1986

16. Kahneman/Tversky (1991): Kahneman, D., Tversky, A., *Loss aversion in risk less choice: A reference dependent model*, Quarterly Journal of Economics, no 106, MIT, Cambridge 1991

17. Kahneman (1991): Kahneman et al, *Anomalies: The endowment effect, loss aversion, and status quo bias*, Journal of Economic Perspectives, 5/1, Cambridge 1991

18. Kahneman/Tversky (2000): Kahneman, D., Tversky, A., *Choices, values and frames*, Cambridge University Press, New York 2000

19. Klose (1993): Klose, W., *Ökonomische Analyse von Entscheidungsanomalien*, Europäische Hochschulschriften (WiWi), Band 1533, Verlag Peter Lang, Frankfurt am Main 1993

20. Mandelbrot/Hudson (2004): Mandelbrot, B., Hudson, R., *The (mis)behaviour of markets – a fractal view of risk, ruin and reward*, Basic Books Press, Cambridge 2004

21. Miller/Ross (1975): Miller, D., Ross, M., Self-serving biases in the attribution of causality: Fact or fiction?, Psychological Bulletin, number 82, Washington 1975

22. Rabin (1998): Rabin, M., *Psychology and Economics*, Journal of Economic Literature, American Economic Association, March 1998, Volume 36, Issue 1, 03/98, Cambridge 1998

23. Roth/Upmeyer (1989): Roth, H., Upmeyer, A., *Behaviour as an expressive function of attitudes*, in: Upmeyer, A. (ed.), Attitudes and behavioural decisions, Springer, New York 1989

24. Samuelson (1965): Samuelson, P., *Proof that properly anticipated prices fluctuate randomly*, Industrial Management Review, No 6/41, Cambridge 1965

25. Samuelson/Zeckhauser (1988): Samuelson, W., Zeckhauser, R. *Status quo bias in decision making*, Journal of Risk and Uncertainty, ed. 1, Springer, Cambridge 1988

26. Schürmann (1995): Schürmann, M., *Entscheidungen unter Zeitdruck – Der Einfluss des Personenmerkmals Handlungs- und Lageorientierung*, Verlag Dr. Kovac, Hamburg 1995

27. Shefrin (2002): Shefrin, H., *Beyond Greed and Fear - Understanding behavioural finance and the psychology of investing*, Oxford University Press, Oxford 2002

28. Shiller (1993): Shiller, R., *Stock prices and social dynamics*, in: Thaler, R. (editor), Advances in behavioural finance, Russell Sage Foundation, New York 1993

29. Shiller (2004): Shiller, R., *Radical financial innovation*, Discussion Paper No. 1461, Yale University, New Haven 2004 [Internet 02.10.2005] http://www.cowles.econ.yale.edu/

30. Shleifer (2000): Shleifer, A., *Inefficient markets – an introduction to behavioural finance*, 1st edition, Oxford University Press, Oxford 2000

31. Strickland (2001): Strickland, B. (editor), *The Gale Encyclopaedia of Psychology*, 2nd edition, Gale Group, Farmington Hills 2001

32. Thaler (1980): Thaler, R., Towards a positive theory of consumer choice, Journal of Economic Behavior and Organization, issue 1, Harrisonburg 1980

33. Westhoff (1989): Westhoff, K., *Expectations and decisions*, in: Upmeyer, A. (ed.), Attitudes and behavioural decisions, Springer series in social psychology, Springer, New York 1989